STEELY DAN

JUST THE RIFFS FOR PIANO

BY DAVID PEARL

Photo by Frank Ockenfels

Also available: *Steely Dan Just the Riffs for Guitar*, by Rich Zurkowski (02500159)

ISBN 978-1-57560-310-0

Visit our website at www.cherrylane.com

STEELY DAN

JUST THE RIFFS FOR PIANO

INTRODUCTION

Keyboard players have long felt a certain kinship with Donald Fagen, Steely Dan's harmonic wizard, whose sophisticated style at the keys is as unique as his voice and just as eccentric. We devotees of the Dan know that it's Fagen laying down the ripe, jazzy chords underneath his smooth vocals. We hear the piano leading the way through a wandering, unlikely progression of chords. We notice the carefully placed arpeggio on the Rhodes, providing the "wink" to the insinuating lyric. We smile as we hear the bluesy riff evoking the bite of gritty street life, or the dreamy chord capturing the cool, elusive allure of the high life. And through it all we wonder, "How is he doing that?"

Although Donald Fagen has referred to his use of extended chords, and the Steely Dan songbooks give us the overall map of the songs, we can now take the opportunity to zone in on some choice riffs for analysis and edification— not to mention plunder. After all, Steely Dan is perhaps the only popular and enduring rock group daring to venture into the harmonic realms of polychords, chromatic voice leading, open 4ths and 5ths, dissonant key relationships, and the like.

Turn the page and explore these rare riffs, culled from *Can't Buy a Thrill* all the way to *Two Against Nature*, and laid out for you note-for-note, exactly as Donald Fagen played them on the original Steely Dan recordings.

STEELY DAN

JUST THE RIFFS FOR PIANO

CONTENTS

Do It Again

from *Can't Buy a Thrill*

Words and Music by
Walter Becker and Donald Fagen

Organ Solo

Donald shows both his eccentricity and his sophistication in this rare organ ride from the early years. Check out how he uses the first three-note motive to ease down the G minor scale tones, then starts back up by transposing the riff in bar 9 up three times, and then peaks in the stratosphere. Bringing the line back down gradually, he toys with the sliding grace notes between quarter note triplets and creates a nice "blurred" effect with those eighth note triplets stepping back down the scale at the end.

Reeling in the Years

from *Can't Buy a Thrill*

Words and Music by
Walter Becker and Donald Fagen

Verse Riff Pattern

Here's the "reel" deal happening in the piano during the verses. Both hands hang on to the A on top, moving in 10ths below. The syncopation is what really keeps the rhythm shuffling.

Bodhisattva

from *Countdown to Ecstasy*

Words and Music by
Walter Becker and Donald Fagen

Intro Chordal Riff

Here we get a good look at how Donald sets one rhythmic chordal pattern against another. As the left hand plays a syncopated figure with the band, the right hand goes schizo, but they finally lock in at the end.

Inner Gliss

Get off the bench and inside the piano for this one. It's a perfect effect for a song that mixes Buddhism and the blues.

Synth Chorus

With your hands interlocked, you can really let this one rip. It's like a rock 'n' roll shout chorus with a wacky six-bar extension. These are the chord changes used for the solos.

The Boston Rag

from *Countdown to Ecstasy*

Words and Music by
Walter Becker and Donald Fagen

© Copyright 1973, 1975 by MCA MUSIC PUBLISHING, A Division of
UNIVERSAL STUDIOS, INC.
International Copyright Secured   All Rights Reserved

Intro Melody

A song within a song, this melody starts out in C, then takes us to F and just as quickly to B♭. Then we're on to D minor before settling in on F. But, yes, the song is in C, as we'll find out. In addition to this harmonic excursion, let's not forget to note the classical trills and ornamental filigree.

0:00

Staccato Solo

Time stands still as the band drops out and the piano is left marching alone. You can get a really nice effect by sliding into the A minor from the half step below, and pouncing on the unexpected rhythmic hit before the final bar. This progression, a kind of minor key blues, sets up the guitar solo.

3:11

Parker's Band

from *Pretzel Logic*

Words and Music by
Walter Becker and Donald Fagen

© Copyright 1973, 1974 by MCA MUSIC PUBLISHING, A Division of
UNIVERSAL STUDIOS, INC. and RED GIANT, INC.
All Rights Controlled and Administered by MCA MUSIC PUBLISHING,
A Division of UNIVERSAL STUDIOS, INC.
International Copyright Secured   All Rights Reserved

End Riff

Here's the little bop-like riff that ends the song. Donald salutes Charlie Parker with the accented syncopation and bluesy grace notes, but he keeps the rock beat.

2:31

Rikki Don't Lose That Number

from *Pretzel Logic*

Words and Music by
Walter Becker and Donald Fagen

Chorus Riffs

Let's take a fresh look at some of the quirky features at work in this early hit: there's the odd, chromatic line into the chorus; the bluesy melody starting on the 7th of the chord and harmonized a 3rd above; the Latin-flavored bass patterns; and the uncommon chord changes and resolutions, like Donald's octave-driven riff leading the chorus to a climax from D to C.

3:17

Moderately ♩ = 116

Bad Sneakers

from *Katy Lied*

**Words and Music by
Walter Becker and Donald Fagen**

Comping Riffs

Although this section features a classic guitar solo, we've got to savor the way Donald comps and fills along. Take a look at all the richly varied chord voicings in the right hand, the syncopations, and the bluesy octave fills. The down-up octaves and open spaces in the left hand send the song into a "2" feel—a heavier, funkier variation on the verse groove.

Black Friday

from *Katy Lied*

**Words and Music by
Walter Becker and Donald Fagen**

Intro Shuffle

Although there are two interlocking keyboard parts on the recording, you can get a good groove going by combining the oscillating triplets in your left hand with the bluesy chordal riff in your right hand.

Chordal Riff Fade-out

Slide your thumb from the grace note A up to the B. Donald creates the E7♯9 with these E minor chords on top of the Intro Shuffle, which uses the major 3rd.

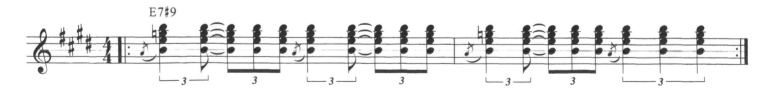

Your Gold Teeth II

from *Katy Lied*

Words and Music by
Walter Becker and Donald Fagen

Extended Instrumental Intro

One of the Dan's prize instrumental journeys, this has particularly juicy chords and colorful flourishes in the piano. There are two 11-bar phrases broken up by irregular rhythm patterns and meter changes, 7th chords in parallel motion, and triads with altered bass notes. Kind of like Debussy with drums.

0:00

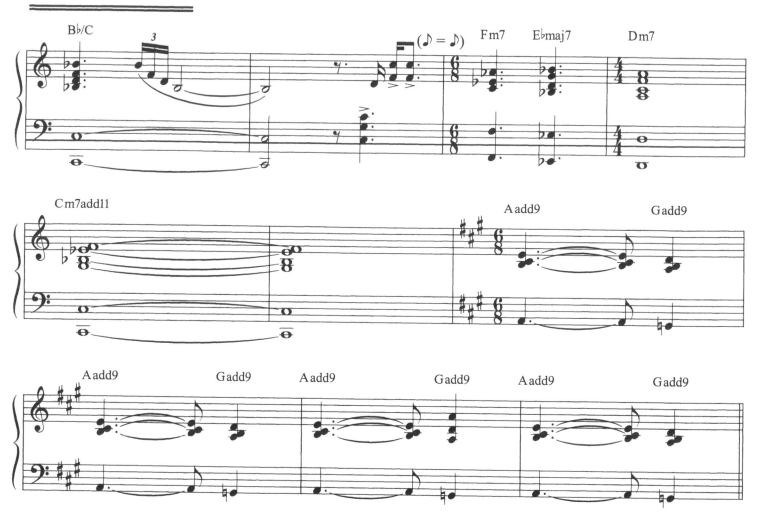

Instrumental Intro Transformed

Here's the same chord progression but with the 6/8 - 9/8 combinations of the verse and chorus, and used as a backdrop to the guitar solo. Always unpredictable, Donald alters the chord voicings and inverts the two-handed arpeggio after the E♭maj7.

2:21

Moderately ♩. = 63

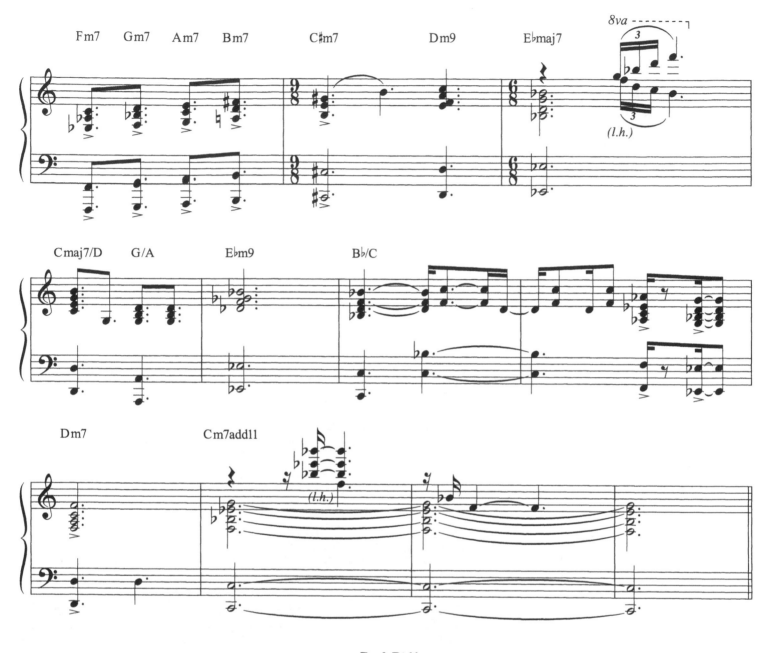

End Riff

Donald throws in a little country riff on the way out. Keeping the ubiquitous "add 9" voicing, he swings down the A pentatonic, finding the common tones while passing the Gadd9, then takes a turn around the flatted 3rd and arrives home on the anticipation. Donald fades out on the gently rocking progression.

3:48

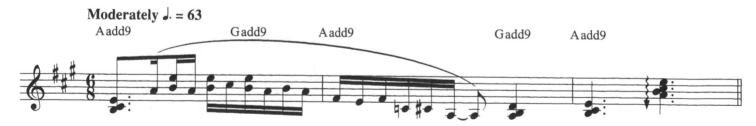

Kid Charlemagne

from *The Royal Scam*

**Words and Music by
Walter Becker and Donald Fagen**

Funky Clavinet Riff

Here, Donald gets that ♯9 chord tension by smudging the ♯9 against the 3rd at the half-step. You'll get the right sound if you play the grace note together with the B♭ on top and quickly slide your finger up to the E.

Release Riff

The tension is released as the ♯9 chords give way to a diatonic progression. Above these syncopated chords, easing down a step at a time, the synth line sings and the guitar wails as the music fades.

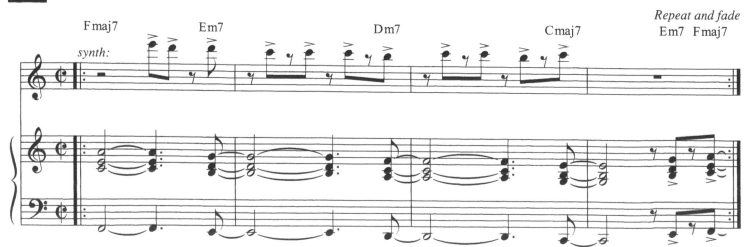

Green Earrings

from *The Royal Scam*

Words and Music by
Walter Becker and Donald Fagen

Intro Chordal Riff

We have a similar use of the funky clav. sound here. This time, chord forms built in 4ths give it bite. Contrast is provided by the triadic voicings in bar 4, which are then squeezed into a three-beat measure, and then we're back to the groove and those biting 4ths.

0:00

Sign In Stranger

from *The Royal Scam*

Words and Music by
Walter Becker and Donald Fagen

Verse Riff #1

The verse is tailor-made for riffing, with a repeating four-bar pattern: two bars of Gm9 for the melody and two bars of C wide open for the riffs. Donald's first riff traverses the C pentatonic scale, grabbing groups by the fistful.

0:12

Verse Riff #2

Same pentatonic outline, but in unison octave lines connected by slurred chromatic grace notes.

0:20

Verse Riff #3

Just when we thought we knew what was coming, Donald takes the octave lines down low, changing up with spare, on-the-beat understatement.

0:28

Verse Riff #4

Now coming at us with offbeats, he's alternating hands and throwing in double time rhythms.

Surprise Chordal Riff

Donald keeps us on our toes. This tutti chordal riff climbs to the precipice on beat 4 and then takes a surprise detour back to the original pattern.

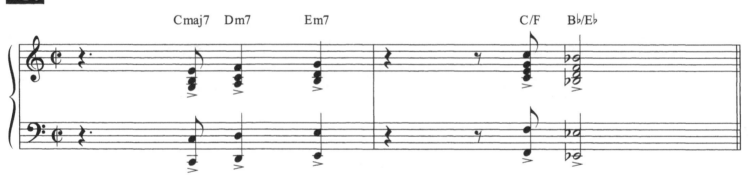

Piano Solo

Now Donald gets to stretch out on the earlier riffs: the right hand is burnin' up the pentatonic patterns double-time, filling in chromatic passing tones; the left hand is playing the in-between 16th note in hand-to-hand rhythms. Look out for the Surprise Chordal Riff reprise in the middle.

Black Cow

from *Aja*

**Words and Music by
Walter Becker and Donald Fagen**

© Copyright 1977, 1978 by MCA MUSIC PUBLISHING, A Division of
UNIVERSAL STUDIOS, INC.
International Copyright Secured   All Rights Reserved

Post-chorus Riff

Using the smooth, crystalline sound of the Rhodes, Donald lays out a two-handed arpeggio on an inverted Cmaj7 chord, building upwards for maximum sonority. The altered bass creates a suspended-in-air feeling, making the transposition of the riff up a minor 3rd feel more like levitation than modulation.

1:23

Moderately ♩ = 92

Keyboard Solo

Donald mixes bluesy scales, bop-like syncopation, and a wash of ascending 3rds in his solo. Notice how the octaves break up the single lines and give symmetry to the two eight-bar sections.

2:45

Deacon Blues

from *Aja*

Words and Music by
Walter Becker and Donald Fagen

© Copyright 1977, 1978 by MCA MUSIC PUBLISHING, A Division of
UNIVERSAL STUDIOS, INC.
International Copyright Secured   All Rights Reserved

Intro Arpeggio

This fits right under the fingers, and with the pedal down creates a nice blur with the #9 and major 3rd
of the chord laid one after the other.

0:12

Moderately fast ♩ = 116

Verse Riff #1

Exploring the pentatonic possibilities of the 13th chord, Donald finds some sweet color-tones during the
verse.

0:51

Verse Riff #2

Later on, more color-tone combinations above a different 13th chord.

1:00

Home at Last

from *Aja*

**Words and Music by
Walter Becker and Donald Fagen**

Intro Solo

Back at the acoustic piano now, Donald lays down a groove by using his left and right hands as a drummer would use the bass drum and snare: the left hand marks the downbeat, then covers the pickup eighths to the upbeats in the right hand.

0:00

Pre-chorus Riff

This riff, played in stark parallel 4ths, creates tension and sets up the chorus. Played with the band in unison, it fuses the verse to the chorus.

0:57

Post-chorus Riff

Here's the release to our Pre-chorus Riff. The soothing 6ths here contrast the biting 4ths we had before.

1:22

Synth Solo

In the middle of an extended instrumental section, we have this rare synth solo. The synth patch is high like a whistle, with a slow attack and a good amount of *portamento* (slurring from one note to the next). Notice how he favors that E natural over the G minor chord.

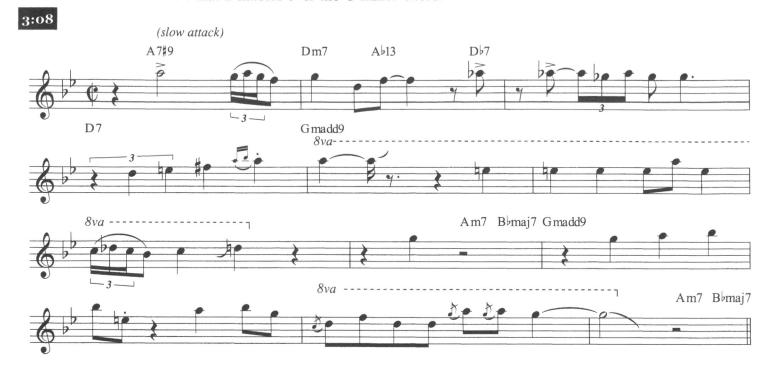

I Got the News

from *Aja*

Words and Music by
Walter Becker and Donald Fagen

Intrepid Intro

The left hand sneaks in, hinting at a blues pattern in the bass, then jumps up to shadow the right hand melody at the octave. The right hand fills in the harmony with blues-note triads. Both hands dart off to pick up a few clusters, then shimmering triplet effects cool down the drama and we're into the verse.

Moderately ♩ = 116

Cluster Chord Riff #1

These spiky clusters dart through the entire song, but we've got 'em pinned down for the moment. A 3rd below the top note, Donald is grabbing minor 2nds, zigzagging ahead of the beat.

0:21

Cluster Chord Riff #2

Just like the blues, we're up to the IV chord and the riff goes up with it.

0:33

Elusive Bridge

With these transparent sounding 4th voicings, the harmonies are even more elusive.

0:41

Stealth Riff #1

We now begin a chain of riffs which follow the Cluster Chord Riff and expand on those warped effects in the Intro. The two riffs here show both hands blazing along, in sync rhythmically, but producing an "out of focus" sound melodically.

0:55

Stealth Riff #2

Here are those blues-inflected triads again, skidding down the C7th scale.

1:45

Stealth Riff #3

Donald uses the flatted 7th (Bb) with a scrambled combination of flatted and natural 3rds and 5ths, weaving a hypnotic spell with the fading triplets.

Stealth Riff #4

We can make out a voicing for a C13 split between both hands, with tone clusters plucked out of it and played in a jerky, syncopated rhythm that challenges the beat.

Stealth Riff #5

Using just a group of notes, both hands have the same fast and quirky rhythm, but like a slot machine, the interval combinations are always turning up different.

Stealth Riff #6

These oscillating half steps again create that major/minor schizoid effect. Add to that the polytonal presence created by the Eb minor chord floating above the C13 groove.

Stealth Riff #7

Once again using a fixed set of notes, Donald punches the rhythms in this riff to emphasize different intervals and chords.

Josie

from *Aja*

**Words and Music by
Walter Becker and Donald Fagen**

Intro Arpeggio

We've seen how Donald draws on quite a few chord extensions to expand the harmonies beyond the typical triads. Here we have three examples of meta-triadic thinking: the stark, open voicing of the D/G voicing, with no chordal 3rd (B), expands out into the A♭maj13, with the F-G cluster having split off from the F♯. Then this new voicing, containing the major 3rd, 6th, and 7th of the chord, is stretched out into a long arpeggio built on ascending 4ths.

First Chorus Riffs

When we look at them in a linear way, we can see in these riffs some smooth lines using the E minor blues scale. When we stack up the lines against the harmonies, we see how they favor the chord extensions and the coolly austere interval of a 4th.

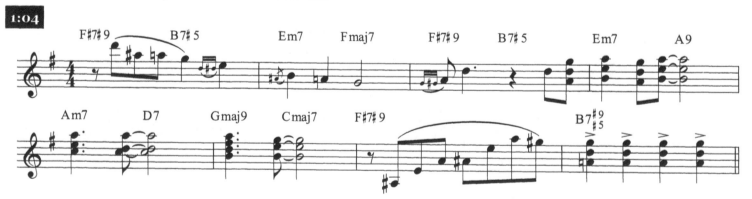

Second Chorus Riffs

In the second chorus he's finding more sweet spots, cultivating the 3rd, 7th, and ♯9 of that F♯7♯9 chord.

Third Chorus Riffs

One chorus later, he's milking those 4ths for more melodic and harmonic sweetness.

Babylon Sisters

from *Gaucho*

Words and Music by
Walter Becker and Donald Fagen

Sparse Intro

Laying out a bare landscape with open 5ths in the left hand and jarring chord progressions leading us who-knows-where, this is one prize intro. In the right hand we've got cool, single lines on the Rhodes, plus cluster chord voicings contrasting those sudden bursts of bitonality as the accented major triads derail the tonal direction.

0:00

Moderately slow ♩ = 60

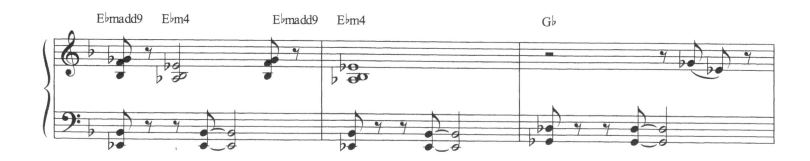

First Chorus Riffs

With plenty of air space in between the vocal phrases, Donald goes for understatement: a pair of 16th note triplet turns, down to D minor, then a parallel 4th triplet, slowed down for a slide into the C13, stacking up those 4ths for a unique chord voicing.

1:25

Transition

We've got those parallel 4ths leading us in, some new triad-over-bass combinations, and later we've got the E♭ minor voicings from the intro stretched further into ever more obscure harmonies.

1:51

End Vamp

Fading out on the chorus hook, Donald teaches us something about using parallel relationships in the chord progression: the new (diatonic) shift up to F from D minor sounds more radical than the (chromatic) shift up to E♭, which was established in the chorus. This switch is just one of the clever additions to the vamp.

4:42

Gaucho

from *Gaucho*

**Words and Music by
Walter Becker, Donald Fagen
and Keith Jarrett**

Funky Amen Intro

Gleaned from a gospel keyboard style, the rise and fall of this suspension-resolution progression is exaggerated by the heavy attack on the backbeat and the understated release on the downbeat. The riff going into the 4th bar, with the grace note pulling down the A to a bluesier, flatter 3rd, makes its first appearance.

0:00

Moderately slow ♩ = 63

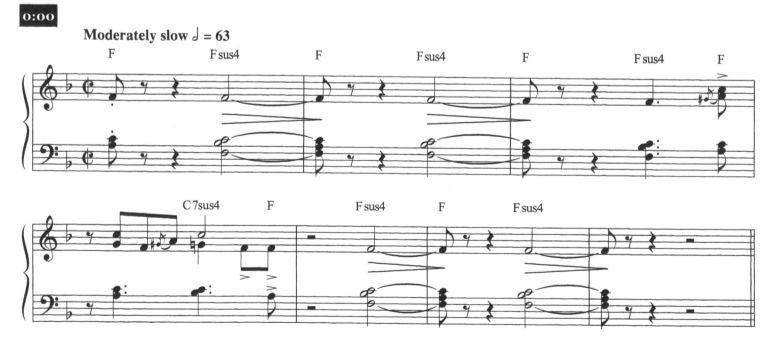

Pre-verse Riff and Cadence

Our grace note-inflected riff now sets up a more final riff—with the left hand harmonizing the right in moving 10ths and 6ths—and builds to a strong cadence, now nailed on the downbeat. But we've got a few low "amen" cadences before we meet the gaucho.

Pre-chorus Chordal Riff

Donald is using the Rhodes throughout the song, but here we have the piano in an overlay chordal riff leading into the chorus. It's an especially nice change of color since the A♭ triad clashes above the smooth E♭ 6/9 chord being held by the Rhodes. The dissonance makes perfect sense: as it overlaps with the downbeat of the chorus it slides up into the Fmaj7. It's that flatted 3rd, flatted 7th blues trick applied in a new way.

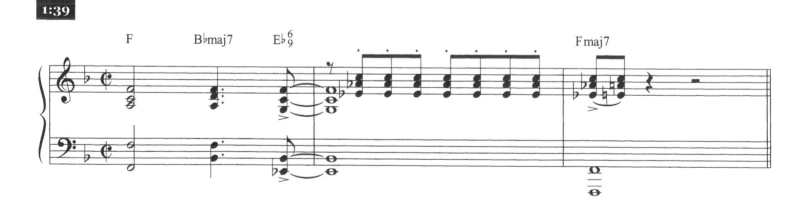

Rainbow Riff

Like an arch of sparkling color, this line shines with the extensions above the D minor chord: the 7th, 9th, and 11th outline a C major superimposed on the Dm7.

Glamour Profession

from *Gaucho*

Words and Music by
Walter Becker and Donald Fagen

Copyright © 1980, 1981 Zeon Music (ASCAP) and Freejunket Music (ASCAP)
International Copyright Secured   All Rights Reserved

Piano Solo

Donald stretches out with several ideas here. In the right hand, he's shading octave lines with blues notes, with a few single lines colored by chord tones above. He's keeping quite a few elements in play throughout the solo, like lines moving in 4ths and the quarter note triplet rhythm. And see how he develops the three-note groupings—those in 4ths, and those filling in a major or minor 3rd. In the left hand, he's using juicy jazz voicings and chromatic voice leading, going from full chords to single notes and creating rhythmic interplay between the hands. Note the six-bar cycle of chords.

My Rival

from *Gaucho*

Words and Music by
Walter Becker and Donald Fagen

Intro Riffs

An ultra-cool organ sound sets the suspicious tone of the tune here. The first phrase sneaks upward, then is answered by another, taken down to mark the peculiar harmonic change in the middle of the bar. You'll want to remember how the chord hits in the last bar leave that gaping hole on beat 4, but don't miss the nice voicing.

0:00

Moderate Funk $\quad \downarrow$ = 96

Slinky Setup

Deep in the background, the organ fills that hole on beat 4 with a low-down riff, setting up the verse. The two lines keep shifting the G to G♯, toying with the major/minor ambivalence.

0:32

Organ Riffs

Talking back during the instrumental section, Donald makes the most of the organ's light action with fall-offs and staccato articulations.

1:59

Time Out of Mind

from *Gaucho*

**Words and Music by
Walter Becker and Donald Fagen**

Copyright © 1980 Zeon Music (ASCAP) and Freejunket Music (ASCAP)
International Copyright Secured All Rights Reserved

Piano Break

Take a ride on this catchy progression and you'll find you can't get off. With its sonorous voicings, contagiously syncopated rhythm, ascending 4ths in the bass, and honky-tonk ending, it's quite a hook.

2:00

Moderately bright ♩ = 120

Cousin Dupree

from *Two Against Nature*

**Words and Music by
Walter Becker and Donald Fagen**

Left Hand Groove

The left hand hits an upbeat groove with a wink to a traditional blues pattern. The usual open 5th expanding to a 6th and then a minor 7th is trimmed here to single notes skipping from one to another with a light touch.

0:00

Multi-keyboard Riffs

Donald is riffing on the Rhodes above the verse, while still jumping on those rhythmically displaced chords at the piano, with some added fill-ins on the upbeats. At the Rhodes he riffs on the flat 7-6-5 motif harmonized in 3rds, shaking and scooping up for bluesy effect.

1:14

C7

Gaslighting Abbie

from *Two Against Nature*

Words and Music by
Walter Becker and Donald Fagen

Intro Groove

A light and sparse combination of chordal and single riffing adds to this funky brew. There's a nicely spread voicing of the E9 coming out of the first two tight voicings. And, true to nature, he's playing with that chordal 3rd ambiguity, throwing in the suspended 4th here and the flatted 3rd there.

0:18

Moderately $\quad \downarrow = 102$

E9

Unison Bop Riff

In this item you can see that Donald has been keepin' up his be-bop chops. How do you know it's Fagen and not Monk? Well, if you had heard only this maybe you wouldn't have been able to tell the difference. But with the line starting with a hint of G♯ minor, then threatening C♯ harmonic minor, stretching the meter out and circling down to G before heading back to an E9 chord, it's got to be pretzel logic.

3:11

N.C.

(to E9)

Two Against Nature

from *Two Against Nature*

**Words and Music by
Walter Becker and Donald Fagen**

Enigma Intro

Set free, Donald takes the cue from the odd meter and lays out some utterly amorphous chords. Played on the Rhodes with the vibrato turned all the way on, he lets us know that nature can be a creepy place.

0:04

Moderately ♩ = 90

Rhodes w/vibrato

N.C.

Skewed Sequence

Ever the jester when it comes to juxtaposition, Donald riffs up the A♭ major chord in the left against the C♭ major block chord in the right (there's that homage to the ♯9 again). Then the whole pattern is set off the bar line like some tape loop that can't quite get lined up.

What a Shame About Me

from *Two Against Nature*

**Words and Music by
Walter Becker and Donald Fagen**

Riff Out of Left Field

Once again, the Rhodes and the piano are Jekyll and Hyde here, with the Rhodes playing the smooth, sustained mellow role while the piano jumps in with spiky, dissonant chords. *Vive la différence.*